LEARN TO PLAY BRAZILIAN JAZZ GUITAR
BY DAVE MARSHALL

To Access the Onine Audio Go To:

www.melbay.com/97746MEB

ONLINE AUDIO

I Choro

Clave Patterns

- 1 Basic choro [:11]
- 2 'Bossa' choro [:10]
- 3 Choro (in style of Villa-Lobos) [:09]

Chord/Rhythm Exercises

- 4 Basic choro [:12]
- 5 'Bossa' choro [:10]
- 6 Choro (in style of Villa-Lobos) [:20]

II Samba

Clave Patterns

- 7 Basic samba [:07]
- 8 Reverse samba—with Ties [:07]
- 9 Reverse samba—without ties [:07]
- 10 Combo samba [:10]

Chord/Rhythm Exercises

- 11 Typical bass-chord pattern [:13]
- 12 Blues/shuffle pattern [:10]
- 13 Choro/bossa-variation pattern [:12]
- 14 Basic samba pattern [:13]
- 15 Basic samba pattern—Changing Bass [:18]
- 16 Reverse samba—with Ties [:10]
- 17 Reverse samba—without Ties [:08]
- 18 Combo samba [:10]

III Bosa Nova

Clave Patterns

- 19 Salsa clave [:10]
- 20 Basic bossa nova clave [:10]

- 21 Basic bossa nova drum [:13]
- 22 Basic bossa nova—in 2/4 time [:10]
- 23 Partial-samba/choro bossa nova [:10]
- 24 Complete samba/choro bossa nova [:10]

Chord/Rhythm Exercises

- 25 Basic bossa nova [:20]
- 26 Partial-samba/choro bossa nova [:33]
- 27 Complete-samba/choro bossa nova [:32]
- 28 Basic samba do-it-yourself [:35]

IV Learning New Brazilian Jazz Music

- 29 Amor Descuidado (Careless Love) [:38]

Brazilian Jazz Solos

- 30 Amor Doce (Sweet Love) [1:32]
- 31 Passacaille (Theme & First Variation) [1:02]
- 32 Bossa Barocco (Bossa Baroque) [:48]
- 33 Bossa Improviso (Impromptu Bossa) [1:30]
- 34 Minuet (from the Notebook for A.M. Bach [1:31]
- 35 Choro Classic (Classical Choro) [1:14]
- 36 Choro Menor (Minor Choro) [1:29]
- 37 De Vez Em Quando (Once In A While) [1:33]
- 38 Marcha Populaire (Folk March) [1:53]
- 39 Melodo de Lua (Moody Melody) [1:44]
- 40 Play the Bossa Nova [1:16]
- 41 Samba de Amor [1:40]
- 42 Samba Sonolento (Sleepy Samba) [1:19]
- 43 Samba Feliz (Happy Samba) [1:26]
- 44 Sonhador (Day Dreamer) [1:28]

TABLE OF CONTENTS

Foreword

Chapter I Introduction

Chapter II Chord Structures and Progressions

Chapter III Rhythm

Chapter IV Learning New Music

Chapter V Personalizing Music

Chapter VI Brazilian Jazz Solos

Solo List

• • • • • • • • • • • • • • • • • • • •

Acknowledgments

I would like to thank Brazilian-jazz great **Charlie Byrd** for spending several hours with me reviewing the early draft of this book. His recollections of his experiences and general comments were both entertaining and extremely helpful.

I would also like to express my appreciation of the combined efforts of two very talented people who volunteered their time and experience to review and edit the manuscript.

Bill Hyder, now retired, was an editor with the Baltimore Sun and holds a degree in music. He now is a freelance writer, lecturer, producer, and an actor. Coincidentally, he is an acquaintance of guitarist Charlie Byrd. When Bill heard I was preparing this book, he was very enthusiastic and offered to edit it.

Liz Williams is a part-time editor for newsletters of several Northern Virginia communities and also prepares resumes. Her full-time job also demands her editorial skills. She, like Bill, was very excited about my book and offered her services. She studied piano as a child, but she found the material challenging and a "good musical refresher."

I want to give a special thanks to long-time student and friend **Ralph Smith** for his enthusiasm and encouragement throughout this project. Ralph was a good listener and always gave sound advice. He was very excited when he first played the samba almost without realizing he had performed it.

This book was a fun project. I simply love Brazilian jazz; it's what made me want to play the classical guitar in the first place. It would not have been fun or possible however, if it were not for the patience and understanding of my wife. Thank you, **Eileen!** This one's for you.

Chapter I Introduction

I-I Brazilian Jazz Guitar Overview

Brazilian Jazz: A Musical Legacy
Manual Summary
Prerequisites
What Type of Guitar for Brazilian Jazz?

I-II History of Jazz/Brazilian Music

Brazilian/Jazz Musical Connection
Villa-Lobos
Louis Armstrong
Jazz: A Description
Brazilian Music: A Description
Brief History of Jazz
History of Brazilian Music

Brazilian Jazz Guitar
Chapter I: INTRODUCTION

I-I Brazilian Jazz Guitar Overview

Brazilian Jazz: A Musical Legacy

By the early Sixties, the nylon-stringed guitar had lost its prominence in U.S. jazz—even the electric guitar was losing favor with the big bands. In 1962, the gentle sounds of the acoustic guitar revived the instrument. It was a natural accompaniment to the melodious and rhythmic new sounds which blended North American jazz and the bossa nova. This new sound was called Brazilian jazz—or, sometimes, simply the bossa nova.

The bossa nova craze came on the world scene like a tornado and was gone by the end of the Sixties. In the aftermath, it left its mark on the musical landscape: **an exceptional, rich music source for the guitar**—both for solo performance and ensemble work. Composed in Brazil by accomplished guitarists, the music is as fresh today as it was at the height of its popularity. The bossa nova may have been only a craze, but it is a music of substance—not just a fad—and, as such, will prove to be as timeless as, say, a Gershwin melody.

Manual Summary

Playing Brazilian jazz requires special musical skills not normally taught to the guitar student. LEARN TO PLAY BRAZILIAN JAZZ GUITAR is designed to provide the guitarist with musical skills and tools necessary to understand and play Brazilian jazz—a one-stop-shopping bossa nova source.

The following summarizes what you should know in order to play Brazilian jazz—with confidence:

°   How chords are structured and how they progress
°   How to play Brazilian rhythms (hands-on)
°   How to master new Brazilian jazz music
°   How to personalize music
°   Brazilian Music—new solo arrangements

These crucial elements are covered in Chapters II through VI. Let's look at each chapter in detail.

Chapter II: Chords

In jazz, you come across some strange-sounding chords like Amaj7 or G7♭5. What do they mean? This section on chord structures is intended to take the mystery out of these. There is no reason to feel intimidated by the seemingly complex names. After all, they simply follow basic rules of harmony—they are not the domain of a 'chosen few.' Feeling comfortable with chord construction often helps a player to find the melody which is usually within the bounds of the chord.

Also, how do chords normally succeed each other in jazz—or other types of music, such as blues? This is covered in the section on chord progressions. Knowing how chords generally flow helps provide a musical compass in navigating new songs—as well as for enabling the player to appreciate the creative task the composer/arranger faces in coming up with novel chord-to-chord flows. It also helps in memorizing a given score: each chord serves as a musical landmark which the melody passes.

Chapter III: Rhythms

In order to put the jazzy chords into proper motion for Brazilian jazz, the player must set them riding on rhythmic waves of syncopated beats. Because understanding rhythms is so essential for playing this music, Chapter III starts out with a elementary coverage of rhythm. This is followed by a description—along with hands-on exercises—of the important Brazilian dance rhythms: the **choro**, **samba**, and **bossa nova**.

Chapter IV: Learning New Brazilian Jazz Music

Guitarists not familiar with Brazilian jazz music may feel a little overwhelmed by its exotic notation. Quite often, rhythm and fill-in embellishments are included along with the melody line. Chapter IV is intended to help you form a strategy for cutting through the extraneous notes and getting to the basic melody/chord structures—a process referred to as 'de-composition.' Once at this basic level, you learn to make sense out of the music and internalize it. For this chapter, you also get tips on memorizing as you master a new song.

Chapter V: Personalizing Music

How do you take an arrangement and truly give it your personal touch? Most musical scores are written or arranged in a style that expresses the writer's taste and experience. They may also be written for an entirely different instrument in mind—such as the piano—or in a key you don't care for. You may also have more than one arrangement and want to merge them into a single best solution for you. Chapter V helps you take this various material and process it into a personal product that matches your particular style, taste and musical goals.

Chapter VI: Brazilian Jazz Solos

Finally, in Chapter VI, you will find a collection of solo guitar arrangements. These are new solos written and/or arranged for this book. They should give you an excellent source of music for personal playing or solo performance. Each was arranged with the guitarist in mind—beginning with key selection—and includes playing aids such as chord diagrams and fingering suggestions. You may want to personalize these solos using the tips provided in Chapter V.

Prerequisites

This manual assumes the reader has the basics of music. If not, there are a number of excellent Mel Bay guitar primers available. This book can be used as a supplement to other materials, such as guitar methods books, music theory, scale pattern books, etc.

What Type of Guitar for Brazilian Jazz?

The nylon-stringed classical guitar is best suited for playing Brazilian jazz. For this reason, studying classical (or fingerstyle) methods is extremely helpful, especially in right hand development.

In Brazilian jazz, there is virtually no strumming, either with fingers or pick. Instead, chords are plucked in very strict rhythmic patterns with little of the sustaining ring, which one gets with a steel-stringed guitar.

The electric guitar is used in contemporary Brazilian music, but usually with other supporting instruments providing the rhythm and bass.

BRAZILIAN/JAZZ MUSICAL CONNECTION

Brazilian jazz is the blending of two musical ingredients from two separate cultures on two separate continents, namely:

- °   The energizing rhythms of Brazil
- °   North American jazz

The two individuals who had the greatest influence on modern Brazilian music and on jazz—Heitor Villa-Lobos and Louis Armstrong, respectively—had similar musical experiences based on improvisation, as well as early experiences performing music in the streets.

Let's look at short bio-sketches of these musical architects.

Villa-Lobos (1887-1959)

Considered by many to be among the important figures of twentieth century Western music, Heitor Villa-Lobos was a prolific composer, as well as a conductor of international repute. He incorporated elements of Brazilian folk, popular, indigenous and children's music in his compositions. He was also very active in developing and promoting musical education in Brazil. He referred to himself as 'the people's composer.'

In his early youth, growing up in Rio, he delighted in participating in the 'choro groups,' which were small ensembles playing in the streets, at dances and in accompaniment to singers. When he was seven or eight years old, his mother got rid of his piano, feeling that he spent too much time at the instrument. Driven to play music, however, he learned to play the guitar in secret. He continued his musical studies, buying and learning from all of the guitar instruction books he could obtain. He studied the works of the great classical masters, working out harmony and counterpoint exercises on the guitar. He eventually got a piano but always considered the guitar his 'confidential instrument.' He wrote more than fifty pieces for the guitar, which are among the most studied, performed and recorded in the history of the instrument.   He generally didn't use actual Brazilian folk tunes but rather wrote original melodies in a Brazilian folk style, developing them in his own manner.

While studying in Paris from 1922 to 1930, he met with the famous Spanish guitarist, Andres Segovia, who was anxiously seeking new material for the guitar.

Segovia, at first, had misgivings about Villa-Lobos' unconventional style, but encouraged him to continue writing for the guitar. The two became friends and Villa-Lobos' twelve Etudes for Guitar, completed in 1929, were dedicated to Segovia—an honor, indeed, considering that each is a concert masterpiece in miniature.

He became the director of musical education in the public schools of Rio de Janeiro, and conducted orchestras in Brazil, the United States, and Europe. He composed about 2000 works, employing almost every form of musical composition: from the guitar solos of his first choros to large orchestral and choral works, varied in their instrumentation, some using the musical idiom of J. S. Bach blended with the intense rhythms and melodic styles of the folk music of northeastern Brazil with its African-Brazilian influences. His works include operas, ballets, symphonies, concertos, chamber music, piano pieces, and songs.

In the late 1950s, while recalling his early days as a street musician, Villa-Lobos said, '**The choros of that time was intelligent improvisation. What is done today with jazz we did here in Rio forty years ago.**'

Louis Armstrong (1900-1971)

Armstrong, popularly known as **Satchmo**, was the first true virtuoso soloist of jazz, as well as a dazzling improviser. In the Twenties, he defined what we now think of as jazz. Before that time, New Orleans jazz was considered to be a 'group effort' played by a small ensemble. Satchmo changed that model by bringing the soloist to the forefront. He showed that jazz improvisation could go far beyond simply ornamenting the melody—he created new melodies based on the chords of the initial tune. He also set standards for all later jazz singers, not only by the way he altered the words and melodies of songs but also by improvising without words, like an instrument (scat singing).

As a youth growing up in New Orleans (birthplace of American jazz), he picked up small change by singing and dancing with other street urchins in the notorious Storyville district. Most amazingly, Armstrong, one of the most influential figures in the history of jazz, was largely self-educated.

In order to get a better idea of how these two musical styles came together, we start out by defining each one, and follow with a brief history of it.

JAZZ: A Description

Dating from the start of the 20th century, jazz is an African-American music that began as a folk music in the South and developed gradually into a sophisticated modern art. Passed on by word-of-mouth over the generations, the three basic elements of jazz are: its sounds, rhythms, and spontaneity.

Jazz sounds emulate black vocal styles, producing nuances of pitch (including blue notes, the flattened tones in the blues style), and tonal effects expressing strongly felt emotions. Its melodies are accompanied by complex chord progressions using non-harmonic tones like sevenths and ninths as basic elements, along with other dissonant chords such as eleventh and thirteenth chords, triads with an added sixth, chromatically altered chords, and suspensions.

Jazz features syncopated rhythms with stimulating, offbeat accents and with swing—a sensation of pull and momentum that arises as the melody is heard alternately together with, then slightly at variance with, the expected pulse or division of a pulse.

It is a basically improvised form of music. Typically, the improvisation is accompanied by the repeated chord progression of a popular song or an original composition. Written scores, if present, are used merely as guides, providing structure within which improvisation occurs.

BRAZILIAN JAZZ: A Description

Brazilian musicians João Gilberto and Antonio Carlos Jobim are credited as the creators of the bossa nova sound. The new sound was characterized as a 'soft-samba' to which was added sophisticated jazz harmonies. The 'soft-samba' is the bossa nova rhythm and the jazz influence was the cool jazz of the Fifties.

Jobim credits fellow singer and guitarist Gilberto as the creator of the bossa nova rhythm in which he recast the samba pattern to an asymmetric beat—a move that upset many Brazilian musical purists who felt the samba had been desecrated by the new musical subculture. They even felt the term 'bossa nova' was some kind of 'hip' Portuguese slang. As a result, Gilberto and Jobim were initially considered outcasts.

Jobim, himself a guitarist as well as composer-extraordinaire, had a genius for pretty melodies with complex chord progressions and arrangements—as such, he did more than anyone to make this Brazilian art form an international sensation. His genius was to create melodies that sing—even seem to float—on top of the infectious rhythm of the bossa nova.

His earliest influences were the wealth of popular tradition in samba and a host of the other native forms which he heard in the streets and clubs of Ipanema, where he was raised, and over the radio. At age fourteen, he studied piano with a German teacher who was an advocate of Arnold Schoenberg's twelve-tone system (which produced music from which any feeling of key or tonality was deliberately banished). He also studied with more conventional teachers. His love for music became a passion when he discovered the works of Brazilian composer Villa-Lobos (who Jobim later met). He was also influenced by French impressionists and American jazz musicians—especially cool jazz artists like Miles Davis and Gil Evans. Jobim soon combined all of his musical loves into an enduring, textured, music that is at once simple and complex. His music is as popular today as it was upon its explosive introduction on the world scene in the early 1960s.

BRIEF HISTORY of JAZZ

Origins

Jazz was developed by black Americans in the early 1900s. As such, jazz is rooted in the musical traditions of West African music and black folk music forms developed in the U.S Other origins include work songs and chants, lullabies, and later, spirituals and blues. Originally a blues was a song of sorrow, sung slowly to the accompaniment of piano or guitar.

Jazz was influenced by European music, Latin American music of black origins, and U.S. music including minstrel shows, saloon piano styles, marches and hymns. Another important musical source was ragtime which is also an African-American music composed for the piano which emerged in the late 1800s. The most famous ragtime composer was Scott Joplin.

New Orleans Jazz

Probably the earliest jazz style to emerge, centered in New Orleans, Louisiana, is a style still popular today and named after its place of birth: New Orleans jazz (also known as '**Dixieland jazz**'). This lively music usually featured the cornet or trumpet on melody, with the clarinet playing counter-melodies, and the trombone added rhythmic fill or simple harmony. The tuba or string bass provided a bass line and drums and/or banjo the rhythmic accompaniment.

Jazz the 1920s

For jazz the 1920s was a decade of great experimentation and discovery. New Orleans jazz musicians, such as Armstrong, migrated to Chicago and New York City. The result was to provide new musical blends which still emphasized soloists, but usually produced more intense rhythms and more complicated textures.

The Big-Band Era (Swing Era)

In the late 1920s, groups of jazz musicians formed into dance bands which became known as big bands. They became so popular in the 1930s and early '40s that the period was known as the swing era. Important names in big-band jazz include Duke Ellington, Fletcher Henderson, and Count Basie. During this period, written scores were introduced into jazz music. As in the Armstrong tradition, emphasis was placed on improvisation, keeping the written passages relatively short and simple.

Postwar 1940s-1950s: Bop, Cool Jazz

By the end of World War II, many big bands had declined in popularity. At this stage, jazz was undergoing a musical revolution. Led by jazz saxophonist Charlie Parker, the new style was known as **bop**. This new jazz retained the use of improvisation, but the music matured and became more serious—tempos were faster, the phrases were more complex.

One of the most influential musicians in the late 1940s was trumpeter Miles Davis, whose music was soft in tone but highly complex and became known as **cool jazz**. Cool jazz was especially popular on the West Coast, so it became known as West Coast jazz.

The opposite of cool jazz was hard bop, which was played in the Eastern cities. Hard bop was vigorous and energetic and emphasized the African-American basis of jazz.

1960s: Modal Jazz and the Bossa Nova

In the mid-1950s and into the 1960s, Miles Davis devised pieces that would remain in one key and chord for as long as sixteen measures at a time—leading to the term modal jazz—allowing much freedom for the improviser. Much of the new jazz of the 1960s was based on these modal structures.

Bossa Nova Craze

In the Spring of 1961, classical/jazz guitarist **Charlie Byrd**, who studied with Andres Segovia, traveled to South America on a U.S. State Department sponsored good will trip. While in Brazil, he came in contact with the new exciting jazzy bossa nova sounds being played there. On his return to the States (music and records in hand), he sought out and introduced the new sound to jazz saxophonist **Stan Getz** who fell equally in love with its easy flowing sounds. They recorded an album titled *Jazz Samba* which, on its release in early 1962, became an overnight hit—almost unheard of for jazz, at the time! By year's end, the bossa nova was an all-out national craze in the U.S.—complete with novelty vendor-generated gadgets, Tee shirts, buttons, you name it! The bossa nova craze reached its crest in the mid-to-late 1960s, but its effects remain. Thanks

12

to Charlie's recognition and promotion of Brazilian jazz, it has emerged from the night clubs of Rio to become a standard music form throughout the world.

HISTORY of BRAZILIAN MUSIC

Some of the early Latin American composers followed European musical examples. The arrival of blacks in northeastern Brazil and the Caribbean brought new musical forms that were later expressed in such dances as the rumba, samba, and tango.

Brazil has a rich folk music tradition that synthesizes elements of African and Portuguese traditional music, and, more subtly, the remaining strain of the aboriginal Indians. The mixture of these diverse elements varies from region to region.

Brazilian dance—such as the samba, maxixe, baiao, and frevo—are probably the most significant expressions of the country's musical identity. These dances as well as well-known urban tunes further flavor the total resources of Brazilian music. To these must be added the songs and dances of Spain, Italian opera, French melodies, and North American jazz.

The most influential modern Brazilian composer, Heitor Villa-Lobos, is also perhaps the most gifted one (see short life history at beginning of this section). More recently, the melodies and rhythms of the bossa nova—first appearing in the mid-1950s—have received world-wide recognition and popularity. Among its leading composers are Luis Bonfa and Antonio Carlos Jobim, who created the score for the classic 1959 film, Black Orpheus. For the film, Bonfa wrote '*Manha de Carnival*' and '*Samba de Orfeo*' and Jobim wrote '*A Felicidade,*' which was the first song to bring him international attention. Jobim went on to write hundreds of songs—many becoming international hits.

Chapter II Chord Structures/Progressions

II-I Chord Structures

Harmonics/Harmony
Single Note
Two Notes (Intervals)
Three Notes (Triad-Chord)
      C Major (C)
      C Minor (Cm)
      C Augmented (Caug)
      C Diminished (Cdim)
      C Suspended (Csus4)
Four-Note Chords
      C Seventh (C7)
      C Major Seventh (Cmaj7)
      C Ninth, C Eleventh, C Thirteenth (C9, C11, C13)
      Mix and Match Chords

II-II Chord Progressions

Tonal Harmony
Harmonic Progression
Functional Names
Circle of Fifths
Keys

Chapter II: Chord Structures/Progressions

II-I Chord Structures

Harmonics/Harmony

Before we get started on the subject of harmony, let's differentiate harmonics from harmony:

- **Harmonics** is defined as the theory, or study, of the **physical properties** and **characteristics** of **sound**
- **Harmony** is the study of the **structure, progression** and **relation** of **chords**; together with melody and rhythm, it is one of the three primary elements of music

Harmonics
Single Note

When we play a single note, an amazing set of acoustical events is set into motion: first, a fundamental tone is produced along with a series of overtones (sound waves whose frequencies are whole-number multiples of the fundamental frequency). The resultant sound waves are collectively responsible for creating the unique tonality of the guitar. This unique sound is referred to as 'timbre.' Timbre is, the quality of sound which distinguishes it from other sounds of the same pitch and volume and from other instruments or sound sources.

Harmonics is also a tone produced on the guitar by lightly touching a string at a given fraction of its length (for instance, the twelfth fret) while it is plucked causing both segments to vibrate—thereby creating a chime-like sound. The chime-like sound at the twelfth fret is a second order overtone and is always present when a string is played. We hear it as a chime because lightly touching the string dampens the fundamental frequency and other overtones, leaving a relatively pure tone like the sound of a bell.

Harmony
Two Notes (Intervals)

The distance between any two notes is called an interval. When we play two notes, the resultant acoustical events are much more complex than simply the sum of the individual events: we get the fundamental tones—and associated overtones—of each note along with additional tones with represent the sum and difference of the original notes. This concept may be of more interest to a sound engineer than a musician. For the guitarist, however, it is important since, when playing multiple notes, **harmony** of some kind occurs.

Intervals, therefore, are the **building blocks of harmony**. Some intervals are **consonant** (the two notes are compatible with each other), and some intervals are **dissonant** (the two notes clash with each other). Dissonant intervals create musical tension—like syncopation for rhythm— which require that they be resolved to a consonance. You will hear dissonant intervals often in jazz.

The rules invented by musical theorists change from one period of history to another. So does popular taste. Therefore, the idea of which intervals are consonant and which are dissonant has evolved over centuries. Today we consider seconds and sevenths dissonant. The rest of the intervals are considered consonant unless they are augmented or diminished. [Don't worry about those terms. We'll take them up in the section headed 'Three Note (Triad Chord).']

Consider the scale below:

The interval between the first note (C) and the second (D) is called a second; between the first and the third (E) a third, and so on. As we know, the interval between the C and the eighth step, also a C, is called an octave, not an eighth. From there upward the sequence continues as usual: the interval between C and the higher D is a ninth, and so on up to the thirteenth (high A). From C upward almost two octaves to a B (not shown in the illustration) is a fourteenth. An interval of two octaves is technically called a fifteenth, though it is more usually referred to as two octaves.

Note that these names are used to indicate the distance between any two notes. If we start with the D instead of C, we consider D the first step. So the distance between D and E is a second, between D and F a third, between D and A a fifth, and so on.

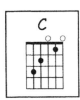

Three Notes (Triad-Chord)

Playing a third (C and E, let's say) with another third on top (E and G) is what is called a triad (see at right):

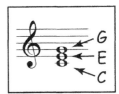

The triad is the basic form of a **chord**. In the triad above, the C is called the **root**, the E is called the **third**, and the G is the **fifth**. (The same terms are used for the notes in all triads.) Other notes can be added, as we'll see. Even when the triad is inverted—in other words, when the notes are rearranged so the E or the G is the bottom note—the C is still the root, the E is the third, and the G is the fifth.

The notes of a chord can be played simultaneously or in succession. A chord whose notes are played in succession is called an arpeggio (from the Italian word for a harp) or a 'broken chord.' The figure below shows many of the chords that can be built on the C-E-G triad.

Harmony: How Chords Stack Up

The first four chords are considered simple triads since they contain only **root, third,** and **fifth intervals.** The first two—C and Cm—are classified as consonant, since they contain only consonant intervals. This makes them stable chords in tonal music, meaning they require no resolution (explained in next sentence). The next two chords—Cdim and Caug—are classified as dissonant, meaning they contain dissonant intervals and, thus, are unstable and need to be resolved—meaning they probably require transitioning to a more stable triad. (You wouldn't expect the music to stop at one of these chords.)

Staying with the key of C, let's consider each chord within the major triad.

C Major (C)

A 'perfect' major chord is defined as a triad consisting of the **root, third,** and **fifth** tones. Looking back at the scale, for C major, the triad notes are C, E, and G. When we play a C major chord, only these notes are played. Some notes may be repeated at other octaves. Major chords sound happy and rather uplifting to Westerners.

C Minor (Cm)

A minor chord consists of the notes of the major, but the third—E for the C chord—is flatted (lowered) by a half step (one fret, on the guitar). Looking back at the scale, for C minor, the triad notes are C, Eb, and G. In contrast with major chords, minor chords seem negative and can bring about feelings of sadness; however, songs in minor keys can be among the most beautiful and expressive.

C Augmented (Caug)

An augmented chord is simply a major triad with the fifth interval sharpened (raised) a half step. In the scale, for C augmented, the triad notes are C, E, and G♯. Augmented chords are normally used as a temporary deviation from the major chord or as a transition chord to another chord. In either case, they provide rich texture to the music.

C Diminished (Cdim)

A diminished chord is a major triad with both the third and fifth intervals flatted by a half step. In the scale, for C diminished, the triad notes are C, Eb, and Gb. Diminished chords, just as augmented, are often used as a temporary deviation from the major chord or as a transition chord to another chord. Also, like augmented chords, they provide rich texture to the music. In some compositions, diminished chords can add a touch of flair or drama.

C Suspended (Csus4)

When we add the fourth interval to a major triad, we place the harmony in a state of suspension. This suspended state—often used as a temporary deviation from the major chord—seems to demand resolution back to the major chord. The F wants to subside into an E (try this on the guitar). As with augmented and diminished chords, suspended fourths provide rich texture to the music, if not overdone.

Four or More-Note Chords

When we add additional notes to the major triads, we create embellishments that until this century were considered non-harmonic tones but have come to be considered standard. Particularly common in this category are seventh chords (additional note lying a seventh above the root) and ninth chords (two additional notes a seventh and a ninth above the root). Jazz and 20th-century popular music use these chords as basic elements, along with other dissonant chords such as eleventh and thirteenth chords, triads with an added sixth, chromatically altered chords, and suspensions.

Again, staying with the key of C, let's examine each chord.

Seventh Chords

There are actually two types of seventh chords: **major and minor**. The seventh note from C is B and is the major seventh. Flatting the major seventh gives the minor seventh chord. Let's consider each:

C (Minor) Seventh (C7)

By convention, when the chord is not qualified as a major seventh—that is, maj7—it is assumed to be a minor seventh, and is simply called a C seventh chord. Minor seventh chords are used for transitions in traditional music. In jazz and blues, they are frequently used as root-chord substitutes.

C Major Seventh (Cmaj7)

C major seventh chord has an added B natural (or seventh interval in the key of C) note. This is an especially beautiful, moody sounding chord. It is used very often—and extremely well—in Brazilian jazz.

C Ninth, C Eleventh, C Thirteenth (C9, C11, C13)

Ninths, elevenths, and thirteenths are formed by adding notes that are at the 9th, 11th, and 13th intervals above the root note. For C, they are D, F, and A, respectively.

Triads and seventh chords constituted the basic harmonic vocabulary of traditional music from the fifteenth century until about 1900. After that, 9th, 11th, and 13th chords gained wider acceptance—particularly in the music of the French Impressionists and in jazz.

Today, we find that jazz (certainly, Brazilian jazz) and 20th-century popular music utilize these chords as basic elements. As a group, they serve to add spice and zest to the basic triad.

Mix and Match Chords

There is a class of chords that are combinations of sevenths, ninths, elevenths, and thirteenths. To begin, minor, augmented, and diminished chords can be embellished with higher-order notes the same as majors. For instance, an Am7 is A minor with its seventh, G, included. It is also possible to alter an added note by raising or lowering it by a half tone. The chord G7(♭5) is simply G7 (minor 7th note is F) with its 5th (D) flatted. A minor 6/9 is just a minor chord with both the 6th and 9th notes present.

Chapter II: Chord Structures/Progressions

II-II Chord Progressions

Tonal Harmony: Coming Home

In the last several hundred years, most Western music has been **tonal**—that is, it has a central, or 'home-base' tone, called the tonic, toward which all other tones seem to gravitate.

You may recall that, in the section on jazz history, it was pointed out that Jobim's music teacher was a proponent of Arnold Schoenberg, who abandoned this sense of tonality altogether and began writing atonal music (that is, music without a tonic). Jobim later abandoned Schoenberg's methods.

Harmonic Progression

The movement from one chord to another, called a **harmonic progression**, creates much of the sense of motion in tonal music.

Functional Names

Chords are given functional names (labeled with Roman numerals) to identify their place in the diatonic scale. The diatonic scale uses only the eight tones of a standard major or minor scale without chromatic deviations (that is, no sharps or flats). It is the familiar: do, re, mi, fa, so, la, ti, do. For an example, see the scale figure in the previous section.

Three functional names (along with Roman numeral designators) that are of importance to us—since they occur in almost every song—are the following:

- ° I   Tonic or Root   ('home base,' the key chord, e.g., C for the key of C)
- ° IV   Subdominant   (e.g., F for the key of C)
- ° V   Dominant   (e.g., G for the key of C)

You may want to pursue the precise harmonic meaning of tonic, subdominant, dominant on your own. Knowing the above helps you communicate with other musicians who use the Roman numeral designators. They are convenient terms since they are independent of key.

Circle of Fifths: Music's Rosetta Stone

The Circle of Fifths provides a useful view of chord movement. The circle is constructed by starting with any chord—C is shown at the top—and finding the next chord clockwise which is an interval of a fifth from it on the diatonic scale.

The Circle of Fifths has much utility for the musician. With it, we can:

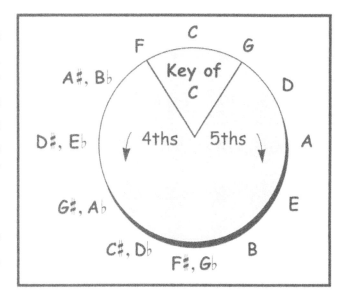

° Show the 'expected' flow away from and toward the root (key) chord

° Determine key chords (they surround the root chord, e.g., F and G for C)

° Transpose chords from one key to another

Using your fingers and beginning with the letter of the initial chord, say the succeeding letters of the alphabet on each succeeding finger. The letter you have for the last finger is the next chord. For example, for C, do as follows:

Finger	1st	2nd	3rd	4th	5th
Letter	C	D	E	F	G

The G chord is the fifth chord from C. In a similar fashion, find D as the fifth from G. Traveling counter-clockwise, the chords occur at intervals of a fourth. This is convenient, since we next address fourths and fifths.

Let's see how a twelve-bar blues progression can be tracked with the Circle of Fifths:

The key is C, which is the twelve o'clock position (the root). As noted in the previous section, sevenths are used in the blues in place of major chords. So the blues progress counterclockwise from C7 to F7 (direction of fourths), then back to the root chord, C7 (home base). From there, we see an excursion of three clock positions clockwise to A7 (measure 8). From there, we trace the chords counterclockwise straight back to the root: A7-Dm7-G7-C7! The Circle of Fifths does not distinguish between minors, sevenths or other four-note chords, such as 9ths, 11ths, or 13ths. On the circle, the progression was simply a generic: A-D-G-C.

The Circle of Fifths can be used in **transposing chords** from one key to another by simply noting the relative chord shift a given song makes in one key (for instance, from C to A above). Then in another key, it will make the same shift relative to the new root. For example, a shift of C to A in C would transpose, in the key of F, to a shift of F to D.

Keys

The following table summarizes the keys normally used for guitar and their associated musical notation.

The **best keys for the guitar**—especially for solo playing—are those that provide open-string bass. This will be further discussed in Chapter IV. The **key signature** is designated by the sharps or flats given at the beginning of the music. The **relative minor** is the minor key sharing the same key signature, for example C and Am. The **first and second bass** (B1, B2) are the (ideal) **alternating bass** pairs you find in traditional music as well as in Brazilian jazz. So, for the key of C, the leading, or first, bass note is the root note, C. This is followed, where possible, by the V ('dominant,' remember?), G. Finally, **the related key chords** are the chords on each side of the root chord in the Circle of Fifths—they are the IV and V chords.

KEY	F	C	G	D	A	E
Key Signature	B♭	None	F♯	F♯, C♯	F♯, C♯, G♯	F♯, C♯, G♯, C♯
Relative Minor:	Dm	Am	Em	Bm	F♯m	C♯m
Tonic Chord Notes:	F, A, C	C, E, G	G, B, D	D, F♯, A	A, C♯, E	E, G♯, B
First Bass (B1):	F	C	G	D	A	E
Second Bass (B2):	C or A	G or E	D or B	A or F♯	E or G♯	B or G♯
Related Key Chords:	B♭, C7	F, G7	C, D7	G, A7	D, E7	A, B7

Chapter III Rhythm

III-I Rhythm Primer

Rhythm Defined/Discussed
Time Signatures (2/2, 2/4, 4/4)

III-II Basic Brazilian Rhythm Workshop

Choro
    Clave
    Rhythm/Chord Exercises

Samba
    Clave
    Rhythm/Chord Exercises

Bossa Nova
    Clave
    Rhythm/Chord Exercises

BRAZILIAN JAZZ GUITAR

Chapter III Rhythm

III-I RHYTHM: A PRIMER

One of the characterizing elements of jazz is its stimulating rhythm. Likewise, so much of what constitutes Brazilian jazz is its wonderful rhythmic textures. Therefore, in order to play this music, it is necessary to understand and appreciate the composition of rhythm—and, more importantly, be able to interpret and play the various Brazilian rhythms. The discussion that follows addresses those aspects of rhythm needed to build a solid rhythmic foundation.

Rhythm: Stress and Duration

Rhythm is that aspect of music concerned with the **movement** of musical sound through time. Webster defines it as: "A regular pattern formed by a series of notes of differing **stress and duration**." We know that when a stone is dropped into a pond, a ripple-effect occurs in which a wavelike motion results even though individual water particles on the surface may simply rise and fall in place. So too, in music, individual notes remain 'in place' but we perceive the note-to-note passages as a musical form of motion.

Using a system which was developed over many centuries, the **duration** of **tones** and **rests** (the interval of silence between tones) is indicated by the shape of the corresponding note or rest symbol. The kind of notes and rests determines their relative, time-dependent relationships (i.e., **beat**): whole, half, quarter, eighth, sixteenth, and so on (each is double or half the value of its neighbor).

A time signature, which establishes the basic pulse, shows how the beats are to be grouped, and indicates a system of **accents or stresses**, is placed on the staff next to the key signature. Vertical bar lines identify the measures (traditionally, the first beat of a metrical grouping is accented the strongest). **Meter** is the specified rhythmic pattern determined by the number of beats in a measure, time values assigned to each note and the unique grouping of musical beats into basic repeating units.

Counting Beats

The most basic rhythmic unit is the **beat or pulse**—a repetitive time pattern as set by the ticking of a clock or metronome. In dance music, the basic pulse is often heard as the constant accompanying pattern of a percussion instrument such as the drum, or piano, or the steady rhythm of a guitar.

In order to play 'in rhythm,' it is necessary to establish some sort of counting method. There is no 'right' counting method—most books differ in their symbols. If you already have a system that works, by all means, continue to use it; however, it is necessary to adjust your system to accommodate the one provided here.

> The method for counting beats in this book is: (1) for notes falling on the pulse, count with whole numbers; (2) for division-by-two notes, count with &s (ands); (3) for division-by-four notes, count starting with the leading beat followed by 'e, &, a.' So, for example, in 2/4 time two half notes are counted 1, 2; four eighth notes are counted 1, &, 2, &; eight eighth notes are counted 1, e, &, a, 2, e, &, a. This may not be clear right now, but will become clear as we proceed with visual examples, which follow.

In the following example, observe the note patterns organized into groups of four (the 4/4 time signature is sometimes referred to as **fox trot** dance step). Using the numbers provided under each note, count as you tap out the note patterns to hear the implied rhythms.

The numbers in parenthesis (2) in the third and fourth measures are included for reference where there is a beat on which no note begins. This occurs due to the dotted quarter notes. Remember that dotted notes increase the notes' time value by a factor of one-half their original value; thus in 4/4 time, the dotted quarter note equals 1½ beats. In Latin rhythms, dotted notes are the norm—not the exception. This creates exciting rhythms, but can be difficult to count. In the next section, you will get plenty of opportunities to overcome any problem you have with this type of rhythm pattern.

Next, observe the note patterns organized into groups of three (the 3/4 time signature is also referred to as a **waltz** dance step). Again, using the numbers provided under each note, count and tap out the note patterns to hear the implied rhythms.

Triplets

A triplet is a three-note figure played in place of two notes. They are encountered frequently in Brazilian jazz.

Triplets can be composed of eighth-notes or quarter-notes. A convenient manner of counting them is to use a three-syllable word, such as ' trip -o- let.'

For example, consider the following:

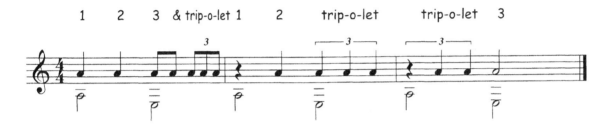

Since two eighth-notes take up one beat, eighth-note triplets consist of three notes in one beat (beat 4 in the first measure). Likewise, quarter-note triplets consist of three notes in two beats (beats 3 and 4 in the second measure). Finally, triplets can incorporate rest notes as in the third measure above.

Accents/ Stresses

Notes are organized into segments called measures. The first beat in a measure is called the **downbeat** of the measure; the last beat is called the **upbeat**—or **offbeat**. The beats in a given measure are usually grouped into a pattern of stresses in which one or more beats are accented—creating what are called the strong beats.

Accents, in musical notation, are usually identified with the '>' symbol. In the following exhibit, the strong beats in traditional, or standard, 4/4 time are seen as beats one and three; while the strong beat for traditional 3/4 time, or European waltz, is the first beat.

As in the previous paragraph, count as you tap out the note patterns to hear the implied rhythms. This time, however, emphasize the accented beats with a slightly stronger tapping gesture.

Syncopation

When a weak beat is stressed, it produces what is called a **syncopation**. In jazz and most Latin rhythms, the accents do not follow the traditional formula of accenting the first (strong) beat of a measure—instead, they emphasize the unexpected: the emphasis on traditionally weak beats create charming and exciting rhythmic patterns.

As seen in the following exhibit, the strong beats in jazz 4/4 time are beats two and four (this also applies to **rock** music); while the strong beat for Venezuelan waltz time is the 'second-and-a-half' beat.

Once again, count as you tap out the note patterns to hear the implied rhythms, emphasizing the accented beats with a slightly stronger tapping gesture.

Compare this syncopated rhythm with its traditional counterpart in the previous section. You will hear a significant difference in this seemingly 'minor' shift of accent. In fact, the difference is significant and helped to elevate rock to a recognized musical form with its driving offbeat, accented pulsation!

In similar fashion, by modifying the traditional waltz rhythm pattern, the Venezuelans have created an enlivening musical form that has become a national passion. You are encouraged to listen to the waltzes of one of the country's most famous composers, Antonio Lauro. Lauro's works have been recorded by many of the world's leading classical guitarists. As is the case with Brazilian jazz, in order to play Venezuelan waltzes, one must first come to terms with their basic rhythmic pattern.

In the next section, we will examine how the Brazilian bossa nova is a 'minor' rhythmic variation of the African-Cuban salsa rhythm.

Time Variations

Rhythm does not have to be maintained with absolute rigidity; it may be played using some freedom which does not significantly alter the basic flow, an effect known as **rubato**. The listener will retain the flow pattern even if the music temporarily strays from it. Rubato adds musical interest and expression to the music. If not overdone, the contrast of the rubato with a return to the established rhythm can be an impressive technique for expressing emotion and individuality.

Some composers, such as Brazilian Villa-Lobos, didn't want to leave the use of rubato to the player's discretion. They often inserted their own pauses—in the form of **ritards, rallentandos** and other rhythmic variations—in their music to indicate where they wanted brief relief from the normal rhythm. The effect, in which the melody momentarily enters a state of suspended animation, creates a delightful musical tension—only to be resolved as the music resumes full tempo.

Tempo

The **tempo** of the music determines the relative **speed of the beat**: the faster the tempo, the shorter the beat and, conversely, the slower the tempo, the longer the beat. For Brazilian jazz, the metronome setting is often ignored. Sometimes, a vague instruction such as 'Moderate Bossa Nova' is provided. This leaves the speed at the discretion of the performer, which allows great flexibility in interpreting a piece. Quite often the title or lyrics may suggest a tempo, such as in the case of a sad love song which should convey an appropriately gentle cadence. Even a samba may be slow—although most are rather spirited in tempo. Listening to a recording can often provide guidance. As always, experiment and find a pace is comfortable for you—this is the ultimate goal.

Time Signatures

In musical notation, meter is indicated by the **time signature**. For example, in the time signature 2/4, the upper number, 2, indicates that each measure has two beats (or pulses); the lower number, 4, indicates that the quarter note equals one beat. Thus in 2/4 time, there are two quarter notes in one measure.

The time signatures most commonly found in Brazilian jazz are:

- ° 2/2 or Cut time
- ° 2/4 time
- ° 4/4 or Common time

Compare the way the note types (whole, half, quarter, eighth, sixteenth, …) differ among the three time signatures in the figure below:

Cut (2/2) Time

For Cut time, the half note is the basic pulse while for 2/4 and Common time, the basic pulse is the quarter note. Brazilian jazz written in Cut time will usually include whole notes to eighth notes. The bass notes usually occur on the beat—as shown—in half-note alternating pairs (C and G in the figure).

2/4 Time

For 2/4 time, the quarter note is the basic pulse. Thus, with two beats in a measure, as in Cut time, notes in this time signature have twice the relative duration of notes in Cut time. So, for instance, an eighth note in Cut time maps to a sixteenth note in 2/4 time. Notes in 2/4 time, usually span from half notes (serves as whole note since it gets two beats) to sixteenth notes.

The presence of the sixteenth note makes 2/4 time appear as if it is to be played faster than its Cut time equivalent. This is not the case, however, since it is the

30

tempo—not the time signature—which establishes speed. In fact, Cut time is quite often used for accelerated rhythms.

The important factor to keep in mind is the **doubling/halving time relationship** between the notes—not between time signatures. It is not uncommon to find the same music scored in several different time signatures. It is a matter of arranger preference. The guitarist should prepare for proficiency in all three time signatures.

Common (4/4) Time

Common time differs from Cut time and 2/4 time in that it has four beats to a measure. Since it has the same quarter note basic pulse as 2/4 time, a given 4/4 time measure will be equivalent to two 2/4 measures. Note that, in this time, there are two cycles of alternating bass lines.

It is also possible to map the 4/4 time quarter note to the Cut time basic pulse—meaning the quarter-note is treated as if it were an eighth-note. In this scheme, the half note provides the two beats in a measure. For all practical purposes, music written in 4/4 time where the quarter-note is mapped to Cut time will appear identical to music actually written in Cut time.

Since most Brazilian music has a 'two-beat' feel, Cut time and 2/4 time are quite often the time signatures of choice.

Chapter III-II: Brazilian Rhythms Workshop

Prerequisite: Rhythm Exercises

In order to master the material in this section, you need a solid foundation in the basic of rhythm. Even if you feel you are proficient in this area, you are urged to take the time to review the information and play the examples in the previous section, Rhythm Primer. Experience has shown that rhythm is one of the most difficult hurdles students face in playing music; thus, the time you invest will pay great dividends. If nothing else, you will understand the conventions used in the exercises which follow.

This is a hands-on section in which you are going to play the following Brazilian rhythms:

- **Choro**
- **Samba**
- **Bossa Nova**

Each will begin with **clave** (pronounced KLA vey) rhythmic pattern—which is explained next.

Clave

A percussion instrument known as **'clave'** can be heard in the background of many Latin dance songs. Claves are two round polished sticks which are struck together. On the drum, it is simulated by a rim shot. Named after this instrument, 'Clave' is also the designation for Latin rhythm cells, which provide a musical 'blueprint' for the percussion instruments to follow—usually played all the way through a song. The clave is a rhythmic shorthand which considers only the accents, independent of melody, chords and other musical aspects. It also ignores the bass arrangement, which usually alternate on the basic pulse, regardless of the drum beat.

III-II Brazilian Rhythm Workshop
CHORO

The choro is a Brazilian dance form which emerged in Rio de Janeiro around 1870. It was the popular music of Rio at the turn of the century, often played in the streets, and was characterized by elaborate improvising. As mentioned earlier, Villa-Lobos wrote a number of choros from his early experience playing in what was called 'choro groups.' It is still very popular.

Basic Choro Clave
The following clave is one of the most basic choro patterns. The bass voice is included since it plays an important role in the overall rhythm scheme.

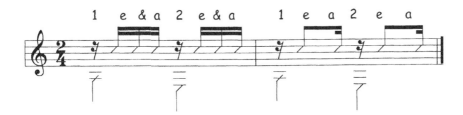

Try tapping it before listening to it on CD track 1.

'Bossa' Choro Clave
Another choro clave—referred to as the **'bossa choro'** in this book since we will see it again in the **bossa nova**—has a modified syncopated meter in the first measure.

Try tapping it before playing or listening to it on CD track 2. After tapping, when you have the rhythm in control, practice playing with just the single 'melody' note and bass—play it first with the thumb and index finger of the right hand. Next, use the thumb and middle finger. Finally, use the thumb and ring finger.

A method of tapping the two voices above is to tap the bass with your foot while clapping your hands for the melody (higher). An alternate method is, using your right hand (or hand you use to pluck the strings), tap the bass with your thumb while tapping your fingers for the melody beats. This second method has the advantage of a more direct transfer to the guitar, once mastered, since you are already engaging the hand which will execute the sound.

Choro In Style Of Villa-Lobos Clave

Another choro clave uses rhythm patterns used by Villa-Lobos. It has the basic components of the previous clave but presented in a slightly different sequence.

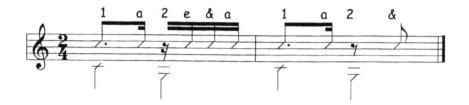

Try tapping it before playing or listening to it on CD track 3.

Brazilian Rhythm Workshop

Choro Chord/Rhythm Exercises

Basic Choro Chord/Rhythm Exercise

The exercise which follows is a choro chord/rhythm exercise based on the clave pattern using only the Am7 chord. Note that the bass alternates on the pulse beats. This exercise is one of several models for rhythm accompaniment. In the first measure, the accent is on each sixteenth note, which is rather straight-forward to execute; in the second measure, a syncopated meter is introduced, making it relatively more difficult to execute. Remember to count and tap first before trying to play. When you are comfortable with your progress, compare yourself to the recording on CD track 4. Keep working at this first exercise until you have it mastered.

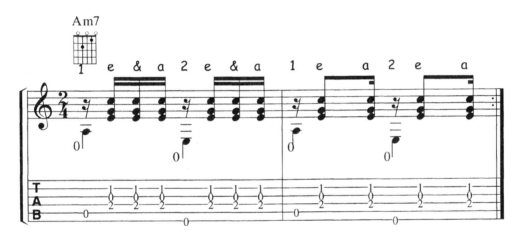

'Bossa' Choro Chord/Rhythm Exercise

The following is a variation on the previous chord/rhythm exercise. It intro-duces several chords, an arpeggio in place of the triple chord pattern and a modified syncopated meter:

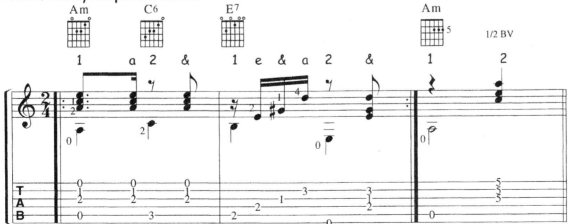

Note that the final chord is Am played as a half-bar on the 5th fret (indicated with a ½BV bar symbol above the staff). This is not essential to the exercise, but provides a satisfying ending. It shouldn't be difficult to play.

Again, try tapping it before listening to it on CD track 5.

Choro Chord/Rhythm Exercise (In Style Of Villa Lobos)

The final choro chord/rhythm exercise is a little more demanding. It is written using rhythm patterns and chord progressions reminiscent of the choros Villa-Lobos wrote in the Twenties (lacking his musical genius, of course).

You are urged to listen to these and other Villa-Lobos works which have been recorded by many leading classical guitarists. It is not difficult to see why some suggest that his choros form the model for Brazilian jazz which came into being some thirty years later!

Note that the exercise begins with a series of three bass notes with pause symbols above them. This was typical of Villa-Lobos (see his Choros No. 1, usually available where classical guitar music is sold). The second measure is quite similar to the arpeggio/syncopated meter you studied in the previous exercise.

Hear this exercise played on CD track 6.

Probably the most difficult chord to carry out is the F#7 in the third measure, which requires a full-bar on the second fret. If this causes you problems, work on it separately—or as a concurring exercise—until it feels natural and comfortable to you. (You don't want to let left-hand problems interfere with your rhythm study.)

In playing the F#7, brush downward with your thumb (note the p symbol for right hand thumb), using the fleshy part—not the thumb nail. The thumb is used for the final E6 chord in the closing measure. Play the B bass, which is accented, in the final measure with a rest stroke. Then, continue the thumb's downward direction with a swift brushing action.

Chapter III-II: Brazilian Rhythms Workshop

Samba

The samba is a dance form that appeared at the beginning of the 20th century. The samba usually has a basic melody and harmony along with a strong use of syncopation. The **'samba feel'** is what could be called a **'two-beat feel.'** More pronounced and driving than the choro, the bass maintains an almost constant **alternation** on the basic pulse, while the melody is often on the off-beat. The usual time signature is 2/4; however 4/4 and 3/4 variations are written—especially in contemporary sambas.

Tie-Notes
The musical notation for both the samba and bossa nova makes extensive use of tie-notes, usually in chords—not bass. This, more than any other factor, contributes to the intimidating appearance of the music, and—more importantly—serves to discourage many guitarists. While tie-notes appear complex and visually clutter the written score, they are used to simply indicate where you hold (or sustain) a preceding chord.

Once you get accustomed to them, you will find they are probably the way you would play the notes anyway. For instance, playing a traditional bass/chord rhythm, the music may be written as follows:

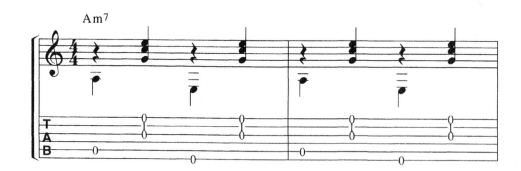

This looks simple enough, but if you play it **precisely** the way it is written, you would have to dampen the chord with your right-hand fingers as you play the next bass note, and stop the bass notes as you play the next chord. **Intentional dampening** gives a staccato sound and is **hard to execute**.

Most likely, you would play the traditional bass/chord rhythm above as:

In other words, you simply sustain the chord, especially since there is no change in the chord. The result is **easier to play** (no dampening involved) and the **sound is fuller**. This second example just **looks harder** than the first. Note that we often allow bass notes to dampen—or decay—naturally rather than stopping them as written (shown above as half-notes). This normally does not cause any musical conflict as long as the diminishing bass is compatible with any melody notes or chords subsequently played.

Basic Samba Clave

The basic samba clave that follows begins with a leading sixteenth note. This effect is used both in the accompaniment and in the melody. The bass voice is included since it is integral to the overall rhythm scheme. **This pattern is often used in combination with the bossa nova.**

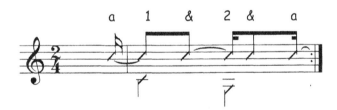

Try tapping it before playing or listening to it on CD track 7. As with the choro, when you are ready, play it first with the thumb and index finger of the right hand. Next, use the thumb and middle finger. Finally, use the thumb and ring finger.

As mentioned in the choro exercises, tap the bass with your foot while clapping your hands for the melody or, using the hand you use to pluck the strings, tap the bass with the thumb while tapping the melody beat with your fingers.

Reverse Samba Clave

As with all Brazilian rhythms, there are many variations on the basic samba. The following is simply a reversal in the basic samba pattern. Note that the leading tie-note is now an eighth note. This is necessary to be consistent with the final eighth note in the second measure (just before the repeat). The rhythm effect of having the tie note is to 'soften' the first beat, since only the bass is played while the chord is sustained.

Try tapping it before playing or listening to it on CD track 8.

Let's now eliminate the leadingtie-note altogether. Notice that the chord is now played on the first beat. In your playing, you always have the option of a tied, softer first beat or the pattern below.

Try tapping it before playing or listening to it on CD track 9.

Combo Samba Clave

Now, let's combine the basic samba and reverse samba claves to get an interesting new two-measure samba beat.

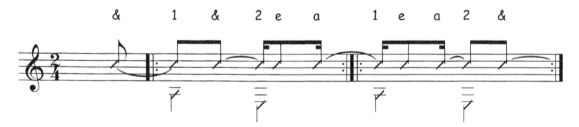

Try tapping it before playing or listening to it on CD track10.

Brazilian Rhythm Workshop

Samba Chord/Rhythm Exercises

Basic Samba Chord/Rhythm Exercise

Typical Bass-Chord Pattern

Before getting into the basic samba exercise, let's take a few minutes to consider a typical bass-chord pattern using three simple chords and a repeating open string bass alternation: B(1) is A and B(2) is E:

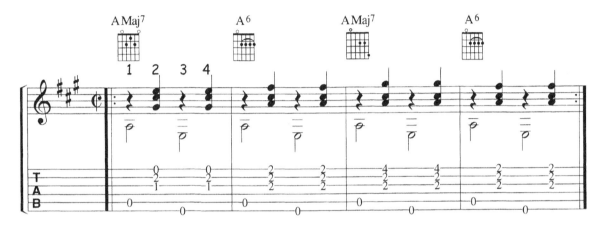

As always, play it before listening to it on CD track11.

Although it is relatively simple, play this exercise to become familiar with the chords, since we will be using this progression in several more exercises.

While there is nothing demanding about this progression, it does convey the traditional sequence of playing chords, the bass is played on a strong beat followed by the chord notes on the weak beat.

Blues/Shuffle Pattern

Next, let's add a little syncopation by delaying the chord notes by an eighth. This pattern is traditional for the blues and is used frequently in jazz.

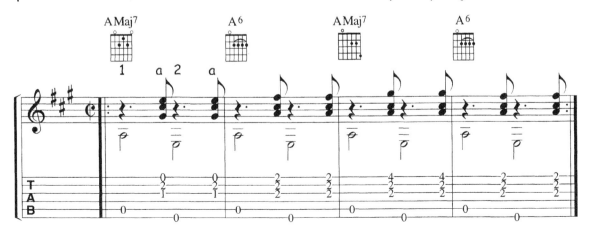

41

As always, try tapping it before playing or listening to it on CD track12.

As you listen and play the exercise, note how the introduced syncopation gives a shuffle effect to the rhythm. You probably will also notice that the chord rhythm has got more interesting.

Choro/Bossa-Variation Pattern
Now, let's use the bossa-variation of the choro:

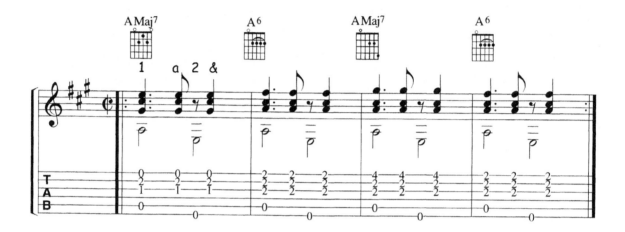

As always, try tapping it before playing or listening to it on CD track13.

The bossa-variation of the choro is can be thought of as a combination of the typical bass-chord pattern and the syncopated blues (or shuffle) example (except the chord is played on the down beat). You may observe that the chord rhythm has continued to become more interesting—a lot more interesting!!

Next, we'll look at how the samba bass-chord pattern is different from the typical, blues/shuffle and choro/bossa.

Basic Samba Pattern
The basic samba does not follow the traditional chord sequence (bass played first followed by the chord notes). Instead, it introduces the chord notes first—in the sixteenth-note at the beginning of the lead measure. This is followed immediately by the first bass note. This pattern is repeated at the end of each measure. When there is a chord change in the following measure, the chord notes must change in the last sixteenth-note of the current measure, as seen in the following exercise:

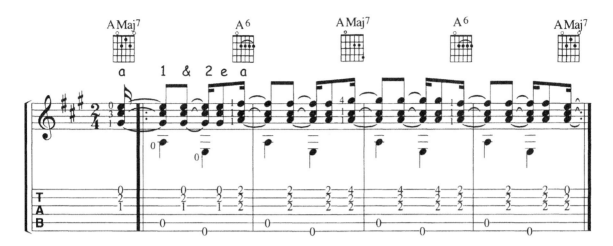

Note that the time signature has been changed from cut time to 2/4 time to give a little variance and practice in going from one meter to another. Try tapping it before playing or listening to it on CD track 14.

If this is your first time playing a samba, don't be discouraged if you find it difficult to perform—that's to be expected. The samba is a complex rhythm. The good news is, once you master it, the pleasure of playing this exciting rhythm makes the hard work worth the effort!

Let's examine the counting pattern for playing the samba: a1 & 2e a1 & 2e a,...etc. The first challenge is getting the first 'a1' pair executed. The action here is a quick, almost snappy, interplay between the playing fingers (usually, right hand) and the thumb. On a flat surface, tap the sixteenth-note with your fingers and say 'a' out loud. Follow this immediately with the thumb and say '1' out loud. When you have this pattern comfortably in control, transfer the action to the guitar. Just concentrate on playing these two beats.

Repeat this process for the rest of the samba pattern. With the '2e' pair, you have the reverse finger/thumb action. This time, using the thumb, you play the '2' beat followed by an immediate chord note, played with the fingers. The action, once again, should be very snappy.

Next, let's study the basic samba pattern with different, or changing bass lines.

Basic Samba Pattern—Changing Bass

To play the basic samba pattern with changing bass, while introducing another factor, need not be significantly harder to execute. In the exercise below, the chords are simple to play, but may appear complicated. Since they are not necessarily the object of the exercise, let's examine them to eliminate any confusion they may cause. To begin, the first and second strings are always open. The first chord, Amaj7, is played at the fifth fret. The second chord, D13, is played at the fourth fret, using the fourth and fifth strings for the bass notes. Note that you can slide the third finger of the left hand down from the fifth fret to the fourth fret to play the C-note of D13 (glide finger).

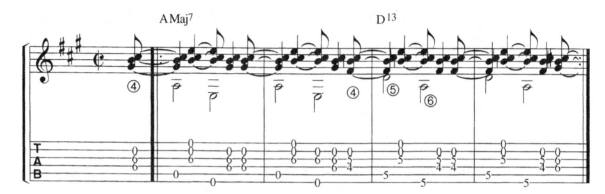

If the chords are a problem, practice playing them without any emphasis on rhythm until they are comfortable and natural to you. As always, try tapping the exercise before playing or listening to it on CD track 15.

Reverse Samba Chord—With Ties

As discussed in the samba clave section, the reverse pattern to the basic samba pattern has a leading tie-note, as shown below. Note that the chord changes at the end of the second and third measures and the time signature is 2/4.

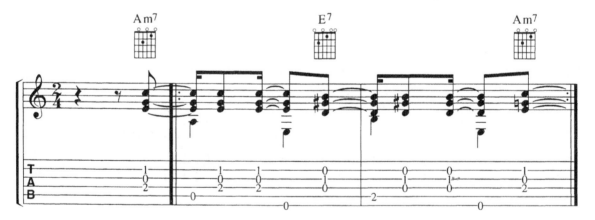

Try tapping it before playing or listening to it on CD track 16.

Reverse Samba Chord—Without Ties

Now, let's repeat the above exercise, but leave out the tie notes. As previously mentioned, you are now going to play the chord on the first beat of each measure. The effect of no ties is a more energetic and driving rhythm, and no chord anticipation.

44

Try tapping it before playing or listening to it on CD track 17.

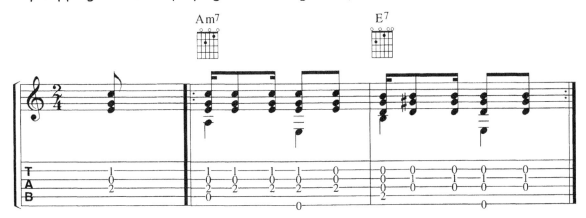

Combo Samba Chord/Rhythm Exercise

This final samba exercise combines the basic samba and reverse samba patterns into a two-measure variation. If you are comfortable with the previous exercises, this should present no new challenge to you.

As always, try tapping it before playing or listening to it on CD track 18.

Chapter III-II: Brazilian Rhythms Workshop
Bossa Nova Clave Patterns

'Shave-and-a-Haircut' knock

In a previous section, we saw how the Venezuelan waltz was created by modifying the European traditional 3/4 time with a 1, 2½, 3 beat (accent is placed on the 2½ weak beat). Let's take a moment to review a rhythmic cliché that just about everyone recognizes as the 'shave-and-a-haircut' knock:

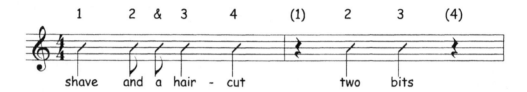

Salsa Clave

Deleting the accents on beats 2 and 3 in the first measure, above, creates an entirely different and exciting rhythm, the African-Cuban **salsa,** which provides the foundation for many musical forms throughout Central and South America. The salsa, rhythmically similar to the bossa nova, is usually played more aggressively than its Brazilian counterpart and has a more complex bass line. The salsa clave pattern takes place over two measures as:

Try tapping it before listening to it on CD track 19.

Bossa Nova Clave

Let's make one last 'minor' adjustment—this time to beat 3 in the second measure, above—creating the **bossa nova pattern**, as seen below.

Try tapping it before listening to it on CD track 20.

The eighth-note shift in the second beat of the second measure creates a syncopation that is rhythmically destabilizing—that is, it no longer ends on a strong beat as in the salsa. With the salsa, the rhythm is resolved at the end of each second measure. This can be demonstrated by clapping out the 'shave-and-a-haircut' knock. Observe that it is complete and rhythmically final.

In the bossa nova, the effect of the eighth-note shift in the second beat is to lead the rhythm forward into the next measure which, again, starts the two-measure cycle. This certainly is part of the appeal in playing in bossa nova rhythm—you feel a continuous, gentle forward nudge into the next clave cycle. 'Bossa' refers to the soft hump above a bull's shoulders, which swings flowingly as the animal walks. 'Nova' in Portuguese means 'new.'

The bossa nova is often executed with a drum playing continuous eighth notes with a brush or stick with one hand and providing the accents as rim shots on the other hand. This creates the clave beat shown below:

Try tapping this eighth-note clave before listening to it on CD track 21.

Basic Bossa Nova Clave—In 2/4 Time
Let's return to the bossa nova clave, but, in 2/4 time. In going from 4/4 to 2/4 time, notice the mapping of notes by one-half, e.g., dotted eighth used for dotted quarter note. Also, the bass voice is included since it plays an important role in the overall rhythm scheme.

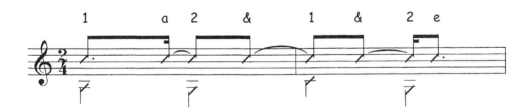

Try tapping it before playing or listening to it on CD track 22. As with the choro and samba, when you are ready, play it first with the thumb and index finger of the right hand. Next, use the thumb and middle finger. Finally, use the thumb and ring finger.

Note that the clave beat of the first measure above is almost identical to one of the choro clave beats repeated at right. The only difference is that, in the choro clave, there is no tie note that sustains the note during the second beat. The lack of a tie

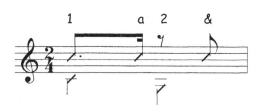

makes the rhythm more staccato—a desired effect for the choro. The inclusion of the tie, however, is consistent with the more gentle rhythm we want for the bossa nova.

Also, note that the clave beat of the second measure above is quite similar to the samba clave beat (repeated at right). In the bossa

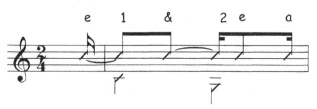

nova, however, the final sixteenth note accent is eliminated—giving what may be referred to as a 'partial' samba beat.

It is noteworthy that the **choro** pattern Villa-Lobos used in the 1920s and the **samba**, which appeared in the early 1900s, found new life in the ingenious rhythm pattern of the more recent bossa nova.

The bossa nova rhythm has been described as a 'soft samba.' You can now understand that several factors contribute to this claim: (1) it eliminates the final accent of its samba component and (2) it intersperses another pattern, the choro variation. Also, it is usually played at a more moderate tempo. The bossa nova rhythm pattern has many variations, which we will now explore.

Partial-Samba/Choro Bossa Nova Clave

Next, we reverse the measure sequence of the basic bossa nova clave and get the following clave beat:

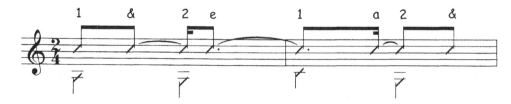

Try tapping it before playing or listening to it on CD track 23.

This new pattern picks up an extra beat (the first beat in the 'partial' samba clave). This is an interesting and very pleasing variation to the basic bossa nova clave. Try using both in your playing.

Complete-Samba/Choro Bossa Nova Clave

Finally, let's place a complete samba clave in the first full measure, a sixteenth note in the measure preceding it and tie it to the first high voice of the samba clave. For symmetry, let's also tie the last sixteenth note of the samba clave to the first high voice of the choro clave, giving the following interesting pattern:

samba/choro clave

Try tapping it before playing or listening to it on CD track 24.

This new pattern is used very effectively in the bossa nova style. You may recall that in the samba section we addressed the anticipation of chord change at the final beat end of a measure. As we will see in the next subsection, this is necessary since, when there is a change of chord, the tied note, or notes, must, in fact, be the new chord. The result, musically, is a stimulating and harmonious device that contributes significantly to the 'Brazilian sound.'

Brazilian Rhythm Workshop

Bossa Nova Chord/Rhythm Exercises

Basic Bossa Nova

The basic bossa nova is used in the following exercise below:

Play it before listening to it on CD track 25.

Partial-Samba/Choro Bossa Nova

The next exercise involves tuning the sixth string down to D (so-called 'Low D' or dropped D tuning). If you are not used to this tuning (or have never tried before), the only two notes that are different, for this particular exercise, are the open D bass for the Dmaj7 chord and the E bass for Em, A7sus4 and A7 chords, for which it appears on the second fret of the sixth string (to compensate for the new tuning). This tuning is a favorite for many guitarists. Once you get comfortable with it, you'll understand why.

The chords are not difficult, but several measures may need some clarification. The B7/9th chord in the third measure is usually played with the third finger barred on the second fret of the first three strings. If this feels awkward, consider a full bar—or some variation you like. The final chord is a harmonic played by very lightly placing your fourth finger on the first three strings at the seventh fret.

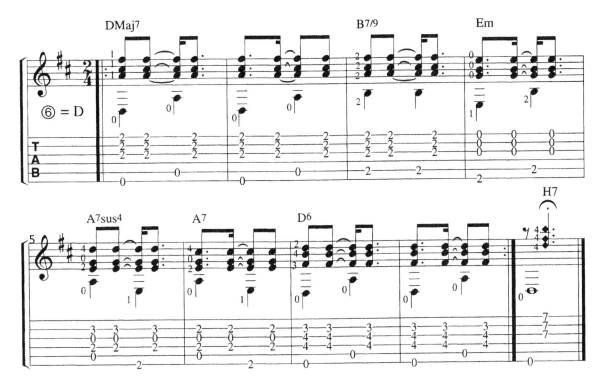

Play it before listening to it on CD track 26.

Complete—Samba/Choro Bossa Nova

Let's stay with the dropped-D chord pattern of the previous exercise and introduce the full—or complete—samba/choro model. All fingering remains the same. Note, however, chords now can change at the end of a measure. Also note that, to add some variety, the time signature has been changed to cut time.

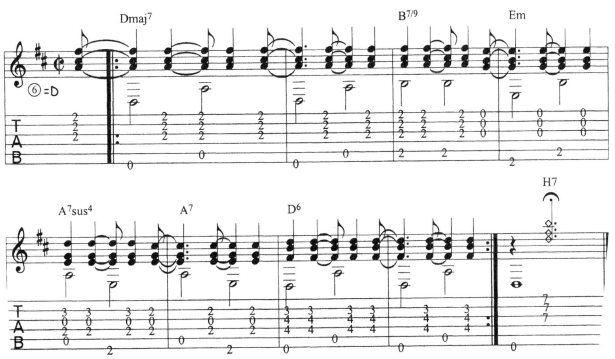

Play it before listening to it on CD track 27.

BASIC SAMBA DO-IT-YOURSELF EXERCISE

Finally, rely on your memory of the basic samba pattern to develop a samba version of the above exercise using the same chord progression.

Use the blank form provided to test how well you have learned the samba pattern. Compare your version with the one shown on the page following the blank form. (Don't look ahead of time!)

BASIC SAMBA DO-IT-YOURSELF KIT

Here's everything you need to develop the basic samba exercise: clave pattern, chords, staff and tab lines. (Remember, the samba is a one-measure pattern, starts with a lead-in chord tied to the first-beat chord and ends with a lead-in chord for the next measure.) If you can't recall it, look back in this section at the clave pattern.

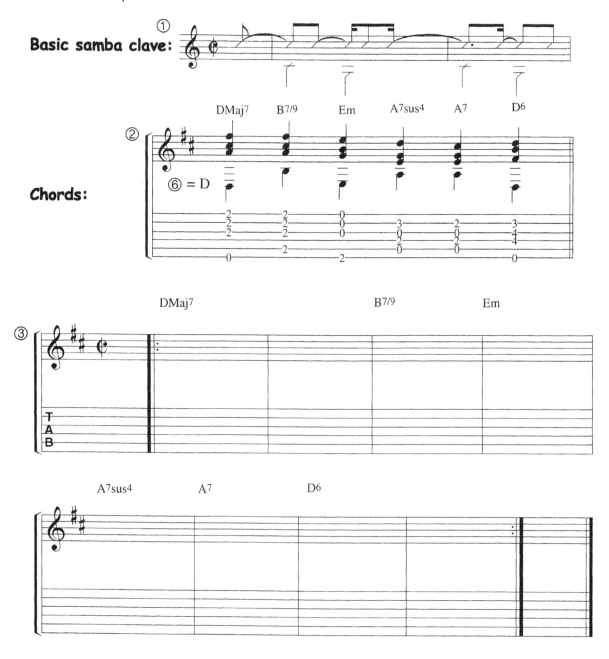

52

BASIC SAMBA DO-IT-YOURSELF SOLUTION

The basic samba exercise is presented in this section to both provide a low D practice piece and to remind you that the basic samba is an alternate rhythm for the bossa nova—for general solo work, and for accompanying other instruments and/or vocals. Observe that in measures 5 and 7 the final eighth note is dropped to provide some variety in the rhythm. If you prefer, put them back in.

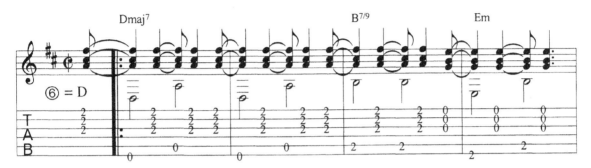

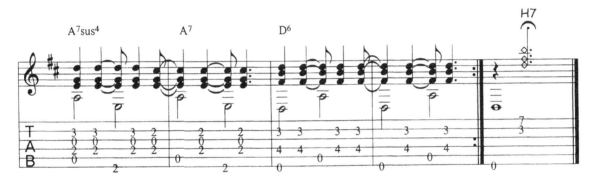

Play it before listening to it on CD track 28.

This **concludes the rhythm exercises.** You are encouraged to devise your own variations on them. For instance, using the chord progression above (or one you particularly like), develop a choro version and practice it. Repeat this with other rhythm variations in this book or that you make up on your own.

Chapter IV: Learning New Brazilian Jazz Music

Brazilian Jazz Music Notation
Getting To Know The Music
De-Composition
De-Composition Example
Starting To Play A New Song
Rhythm Study
Musical Project

Chapter IV: Learning New Brazilian Jazz Music

Brazilian Jazz Music Notation

Traditional music is often written in common time (4/4) or waltz time (3/4). The chords are conventional, consisting of majors, minors, and sevenths. There may be some diminished and augmented chords, and perhaps a major seventh. The rhythm usually has a normal accent on the beat. In general, it is understandable and can be learned in a relatively short time.

U.S. jazz differs from traditional music in that it uses chord embellishments almost exclusively (9ths, 11ths, 13ths. etc.) and the rhythm is usually syncopated. These factors make it more difficult to sight read and play.

Brazilian jazz, like its U.S. counterpart, uses chord embellishments along with even more syncopated rhythm—an extra degree of complexity, which introduces an added obstacle to playing at first reading.

Get To Know The Music

If you are good at sight reading, and have no particular problem playing the music, all well and good. But if you need some additional assistance in interpreting and playing Brazilian jazz solos, it is helpful to get to know the song first. There are several resources available to the guitarist for 'getting to know the song,' namely:

° **Listen to recordings**, not necessarily instrumental only. Vocals and jazz interpretations can help you gain new insight into the music. For guitar, Charlie Byrd has recorded an extensive set of Brazilian jazz both with small combos and orchestra.

° **Piano scores** can be a help because they include a voice staff with lyrics, chords, piano accompaniment, and bass (you have to know bass clef). The drawbacks are they may be in the wrong key and you must be familiar with piano notation.

° **Compare multiple guitar arrangements.** Often, a second or, even, third interpretation can help you understand the song better and expand your alternatives.

De-Composition

When arranging, one usually starts with the basic melody and chord designations. Next, bass notes are determined, followed by the harmonic and rhythmic embellishments. By the end of this tedious and iterative process, the arranger has a solid understanding of the music and, hopefully, has produced an arrangement that pleases.

When we look at a song fully arranged, we lack the understanding that comes from intellectual involvement. The goal of **de-composing** (or de-arranging) is to work backwards to the basic melody/chord structure in order to arrive at a fundamental feeling for the music. From that vantage point, one has a better appreciation for the embellishments, as well as a better foundation for conceiving variations and improvising.

The most direct way of accomplishing this is to study the voice staff, if present (usually found in most piano scores and in some guitar solo collections). If it is not included in the arrangement, you may have to painstakingly dissect the arrangement. If lyrics are provided, they may offer basic melody/rhythm clues. Another source is recordings—vocal and/or instrumental.

De-Composition Example

Consider an example that has been adapted for Brazilian rhythm, **Careless Love**, an early North American folk blues tune. The voice staff was taken from a piano score. Compare the voice staff notes and associated lyrics with the syncopated adaptation in the staff above.

Notice that beginning with the word "Love," there is a dotted whole note. This is a long time for the music to suspend while waiting for the next note at the word "oh." So, a rhythm fill is provided or suggested, since you have the opportunity to provide your own variation. In the next measure of the voice staff, the even rhythm of the four quarter notes are modified in the top staff to provide a Brazilian flavor. In the remaining two measures, a rhythm-fill is substituted for the tied whole and half notes (another opportunity for change).

Now, review the remaking of Careless Love at the basic melody/rhythm stage of arrangement. Listen to it on Track 29. Try introducing new chords and rhythms. Finalize the arrangement by adding harmony. Clearly, the possibilities are endless. Consider developing a traditional or jazz version of the original followed by a syncopated Brazilian rendition.

Starting To Play A New Song

Begin your period of familiarization by **playing only the melody** and, perhaps the **bass line**. In Brazilian jazz, the melody is most important and should be clearly heard above the other notes. This is how you get to really know the melody, especially if it is totally unknown to you. While getting acquainted with the melody, you also learn what chords are involved and their progression. A bonus is you are starting the important process of **memorizing** the song. It is a good idea, at this stage, to **sing the words or hum the melody** (out loud preferred, but not essential) as you accompany yourself. This can really put you on the fast track to understanding the song as well as giving you a heightened sense of confidence in playing it.

Rhythm Study

When learning new music, concentration on the rhythmic patterns can be reduced when attention is given to other factors such as the melody or proper fingering. Thus, it is important to approach all rhythm study **away from the instrument** before playing. This assures total concentration on the rhythm patterns. Mark difficult timing with a pencil and tap out the rhythm patterns. When they feel comfortable to you, pick up the instrument. Experience shows that if you have mastered the rhythm 'feel' in this manner, it can be transferred almost immediately to the guitar. Remember, the habits formed in early practice of a new piece of music can be hard to break later on, so strive to get them right.

Musical Project

Sometimes, it is easy to get discouraged when you don't get immediate satisfaction from a new song. It may help if you think of a song-in-progress as a **project**. A project is a planned process or undertaking for achieving some desired goal. You don't have to declare victory (or defeat) instantly. As a **work in progress**, you constantly refine those difficult passages, enjoy a well-executed phrase, consider obstacles as **temporary** roadblocks to be overcome as you move toward your goal of mastering the work.

Amor Descuidado
(Careless Love)

Adapted and arranged by Dave Marshall

Early North American Folk Blues

Love, _____ oh love, oh care - less love, _____

Love, _____ oh love, oh care - less love, _____

_____ Oh it's love, _____ oh love, _____ oh

care _____ - less love, _____ You _____ see _____ what

care - less love has done. _____

Chapter V: Personalizing Music

Do-It-Yourself Arrangements
Musical Software
Making Your Mark
Chord/Key Considerations
Improvisation
Endings

Chapter V: Personalizing Music: A Personal View

Do-It-Yourself Arrangements

Since most musical scores are written or arranged expressing the writer's taste and experience, you are not always going to be happy with what the arranger came up with. How do you take an arrangement and truly give it your personal touch? One solution is to do your own arranging. As with most other areas in music, there are a number of specialty books which offer advice on this subject.

One of the best resources for self-arranging is the **original piano score**. Piano scores give you all the necessary musical information (most complete with guitar chords) without having the bias of showing a guitar solution that someone else made. Sometimes, we can arrive at a more satisfying product starting from scratch than when we try to re-fashion an existing guitar adaptation.

Musical Software

Today, there are relatively inexpensive musical software products on the market which are, in effect, word processors for writing music. By pressing a button, with these products, you can change key signature, time signature, and pitch, copy sections, delete sections, add/delete measures, etc. Anyone thinking of 'rolling-their-own' arrangements should look into such a product.

In looking for an arrangement of 'Samba de Orfeo' by Luiz Bonfa, for instance, I found several possibilities. One version was in the key of D, but in the second position—too low for any reasonable bass notes. Two others (one the piano score) were in the key of C—the bass situation just got worse, down by a full tone. I knew from an old Chesky jazz album that Bonfa played it in D, but up on the tenth fret. This worked well for him since he had good cymbal and drum work behind him. I wanted a **stand-alone solo**. So, I took the piano version and **entered the melody line and chords into the computer**. I merely pressed a few keys and the music software **instantly transposed** the score into a new key (both melody and chords change automatically). I repeated this process for several other keys and printed out the music in these new keys. I tried each with my guitar. Within an hour, I was convinced that the key of A works best (at least, for me). I then concentrated on arranging this 'key-of-A' version for guitar solo.

Making Your Mark—The Old-Fashioned Way

You don't need to do your own arranging or work with a computer. There are a number of options for you. First and foremost, get in the habit of marking your music. Each guitarist approaches a given piece in a very different and personal way. Make your music the way you want it. Use a pencil—not pen—to annotate. Mark all problem passages, giving both left and, maybe, right-hand fingering and string number. Note any special effects you want to create, such as a metallic sound, slurs, etc. As you get to know a given piece, update any changes in your playing on the sheet. You will find that this will not only assure that you play (and practice) consistently, it will also allow you, should you abandon the song, to return and pick up as you left it, thereby minimizing the re-learning effort.

Be sure to understand the reasoning behind the left-hand fingering and string selection for a given chord before you discard it for your own version. Often, the arranger had reasons for such suggestions, such as tone coloration, preparation for the next measure, and so on. On the other hand, you shouldn't blindly follow a given arrangement, since what works for the person arranging may not suit your skills, taste or the effect you may wish to create.

For favorite songs, try to get several arrangements and, using one as a master sheet, mark up the best approach among them—or the approach that works best for you. This can be a fun project and it allows you to see how differently each guitarist/arranger views a given work. Some favor maximizing open strings while others shy away from them. The bass lines can be quite different among arrangements. If you favor lows, pencil them in—you can always change your mind later. Above all else, be prepared to change your mind about a particular measure, phrase, or, maybe, major section of the music.

Chord/Key Considerations

As discussed above, sometimes a new approach can revitalize an otherwise ho-hum piece for you. If you really like the work but things don't click no matter what changes you bring, look for arrangements in another key—or make the transposition yourself. Here are some thoughts you may want to consider:

Why Choose a Certain Key?
- Key and associated chords known and comfortable for you to play in
- Right pitch for singing voice
- Chords and/or bass notes are open—not closed (i.e., no need to bar)
- Fits well for the type of song
- Provides good solo possibilities
- Good for hammer-ons and pull-offs

Chord/Key Considerations
- In general, for the guitar, the most popular keys are: F, C, G, D, A, and E major; and Am, Dm, and Em
- Open chords usually work best for solo performance (rules out flatted keys: Bb, Eb, Ab, Db, Gb)
- Closed chords can work well for many jazz and some blues and pop numbers—especially if a staccato—or clicking—strum technique is desired.

Chord/Key Options
- Use the Circle of Fifths to transpose chords to another key (pencil them in above score or lyrics)
- Computer software available (less than $50) which can transpose score, chords to any key
- Apply the capo—for instance, with the capo on the 2nd fret, you can use key-of-C chords while, pitch-wise, playing in D

Improvisation

Jazz improvisation means spontaneously playing variations on the melody within the song's chord progression. This implies a degree of freedom—which is not a mandatory prerequisite. Not everyone can, or wants, to improvise. There is nothing to prevent you from performing set arrangements. If you want to experiment with improvisation, as with so many other musical subjects, there are numerous books in the shops devoted to the jazz guitarist. Often, an experienced jazz performer will use known and tested formulas in ways and styles that make it appear (or sound) as if the musical thought had suddenly appeared on the spot—a great gift, and very entertaining. There are no rules against **writing** your improvisational ideas and even **practicing** them—in advance!! You may find that you have a knack for off-the-cuff melodic—or even rhythmic— variations.

> **GOOD NEWS!**
> You don't have to improvise to play Brazilian jazz!

Endings

I especially enjoy experimenting with **introductions and endings**. My approach is to **get off by myself** and begin what I call a musical **'stream-of-consciousness'** playing. The result can sometimes—not always—be a kind of **brainstorming** session in which it seems my hands are in command and I'm mentally in 'neutral gear.' During a few seemingly rare moments, I play something new or different that I've never heard before—something I feel my fingers made up (because I wasn't thinking it). I continue to explore these 'new sounds' and use them for a period of time—a week or two. If I still like them, I write them down. Maybe this technique could work for you.

Chapter VI: Brazilian Jazz Solos

Notation
Chord Symbols
Bossa Nova Style
Solo Study Tips

Solo List

CD Track

30	*AMOR DOCE (Sweet Love)*
31	*PASSACAILLE (Theme & First Variation)*
32	*BOSSA BAROCCO (Bossa Baroque)*
33	*BOSSA IMPROVISO (Impromptu Bossa)*
34	*MINUET (from the Notebook for A.M. Bach)*
35	*CHORO CLASSIC (Classical Choro)*
36	*CHORO MENOR (Minor Choro)*
37	*DE VEZ EM QUANDO (Once In A While)*
38	*MARCHA POPULAIRE (Folk March)*
39	*MELODO DE LUA (Moody Melody)*
40	*PLAY THE BOSSA NOVA*
41	*SAMBA DE AMOR (Samba of Love)*
42	*SAMBA SONOLENTO (Sleepy Samba)*
43	*SAMBA FELIZ (Happy Samba)*
44	*SONHADOR (Day Dreamer)*

Chapter VI: Brazilian Jazz Solos

Notation

As with most Brazilian guitar solo arrangements, the solos in this book use standard classical guitar musical notation such as:

° numbers 1, 2, 3, 4 to indicate left hand placement for index, middle, ring, and small finger

° letters *p, i, m, a, c* to indicate right hand placement for thumb, index, middle, ring, and small finger

° numbers placed in circles to indicate the suggested string for playing a note, where '1' is the high E string and '6' is the low

° bar positions are given with the letter 'B' followed by the Roman numeral of the fret to be barred. Fractions are provided for partial bars

The use of the small finger is not conventional for classical guitar, it is, however, used in flamenco—especially in strumming rasgueados—and for jazz guitar where five-note chords, including bass, are plucked. Note: If you don't normally use c, or don't wish to develop it, then selectively eliminate one of the notes from any five-note chord encountered (usually, a middle voice, certainly not the highest which may be conveying the melody). The result is minimal loss in musical texture. Another option is play the five-note chords with a quick brush downward with the RH thumb—you will find this approach in this collection of solos.

Chord Symbols

Chord symbols are also standard notation. When a specific bass note is suggested, the chord symbol is followed with a 'forward slash' ('/') and the bass note.

Bossa Nova Style

The bossa nova should be played in a very **relaxed, unpretentious** style. The **melody is most important** and should be clearly heard above the other notes; however, the melody is played with freedom (as discussed earlier, retards, rubato, and other tempo variations are used extensively in Brazilian music). Playing Brazilian jazz solos demands that the guitarist maintain a **clear, strong melody** line while providing **solid bass/rhythm** backup. The rhythm may have to subside in some passages, but return frequently enough to sustain the sense of a continuous beat. **Bossa nova accompaniment** should be understated while persistent; it should not compete with other instruments or any vocals.

Solo Study Tips

The following list summarizes points made in Chapters IV and V:

Solo Prep Tips

° Begin by playing only the melody, and, perhaps, a few chords
° Sing the words or hum the melody
° Study rhythm away from the instrument first before playing
° Add your personal touch by marking changes that suit you.

AMOR DOCE
(Sweet Love)

Dave Marshall

Passacaillie (Baroque Theme and Variations)

The origins of the word "baroque" may have been derived from a medieval philosophical term connoting the ridiculous or the strange, or from the Portuguese **barocco** or the Spanish **barueco** to indicate an irregularly shaped pearl. The baroque period evolved in Europe from about 1550 to 1700. By the end of the 18th century, baroque was regularly dismissed as too bizarre or strange to merit serious study.

Baroque composers were quite experimental with chord structures. In this regard, they were ahead of their time. In the Victorian era, performers were known to replace 'dissonant' baroque chords with the more 'proper' equivalents. It has only been since the beginning of the twentieth century that chord embellishments have gained wide musical acceptance—mainly due to the French impressionists and jazz (which also helped to reestablish the art of improvisation).

Weiss' **Passacaillie** was written for the lute (the modern guitar did not exist in his time). It is a baroque dance that was often in the form of a theme and variation. The composer was famed lutenist **Sylvius Leopold Weiss**. Weiss was a contemporary and friend of Bach and is said to have competed with him in improvisation. Some scholars believe Bach wrote his four lute suites for Weiss.

Passacaillie is presented in this book as an example from the guitar repertoire that is strikingly similar in form to modern musical tastes. The arrangement that follows is for the theme and first variation—to show an example of how baroque composers, like jazz composers today, improvised on a given chord/melody pattern.

The trill, which appears in measures seven and fourteen, is played with a repeated pull-off on the first string, starting with F♯ at the second fret, as shown at the right:

PASSACAILLE
(Theme & First Variation)

Arranged by Dave Marshall

Sylvius Leopold Weiss (1668-1750)

BOSSA BAROCCO (Baroque Bossa)

Bossa Baroque, the reworking of **Passacaillie**, is mainly with the rhythm, since the basic chord structures are quite consistent with the Brazilian jazz form. Baroque ornamental embellishments such as trills are omitted.

There are alterations in the case of pure major chords (rare for Brazilian jazz). For instance, Dmaj7 was substituted for D major written for the first and last measures. The Dmaj7 appearing in the fifth measure, however, was Weiss' written chord. Weiss places the major seventh note (C♯) in the bass, instead of the usual practice of including it in the higher notes. The result is very pleasing (at least to modern ears).

BOSSA BARROCO
(Barogue Bossa)

Adapted for bossa nova by
Dave Marshall

Silvius Leopold Weiss (1668-1750)

This page was left blank to
avoid awkward page turns.

BOSSA IMPROVISO
(Impromptu Bossa)

Intro Slow

Dave Marshall

This page was left blank to
avoid awkward page turns.

Minuet in G

The minuet was originally a rustic peasant dance that became the rage among the French aristocracy in the latter half of the seventeenth century.

The arrangement that follows is Johann Sebastian Bach's *Minuet* in G, from the ***Notebook for Anna Magdalena***. Bach wrote a collection of these simple, but charming, instructional keyboard pieces for his second wife, Anna Magdalena. They include arias, marches and other musical types.

Bach (1685-1750) was a German organist and composer of the baroque era, considered by many to be one of the greatest and most productive geniuses in the history of Western music. As mentioned in Chapter I, Villa-Lobos used the musical idiom of Bach. He blended it with the intense rhythms and melodic styles of the folk music of northeastern Brazil with its Afro-Brazilian influences.

Although Bach, like his friend Weiss, did not know the guitar, much of his music plays well on the instrument. The *Minuet in G* is no exception.

MINUET
(from the Notebook for
Anna Magdalena Bach)

Arranged by Dave Marshall

Johann Sebastian Bach
(1685-1750)

CHORO CLASSICAL

Choro Classical is an adaptation Bach's *Minuet in G* to the choro rhythm form. In adapting this particular piece for the choro, it was necessary to map from the original three-quarter meter to cut time. The original rhythm pattern is:

The chosen choro rhythm pattern is:

Play this syncopated version of Bach's delightful work in a crisp, lively manner.

CHORO CLASSICO
(Classical Choro)

Adapted for choro by
Dave Marshall

Johann Sebastian Bach
(1685-1750)

CHORO MENOR
(Minor Choro)

Dave Marshall

DE VEZ EM QUANDO
(Once In A While)

Moderate Bossa

Dave Marshall

MARCHA POPULAIRE (Folk March)

This solo is a liberal interpretation of the second movement (marked Allegretto) of Beethoven's Seventh Symphony. It was composed in 2/4 time and is in the spirit of a march. First performed in Vienna in 1813, Beethoven considered this symphony to be among his finest (most observers today would give equal credence to all of his nine symphonies).

After the first performance of this work in Leipzig, Germany, the audience seemed to be perplexed by the relentless rhythm patterns of the work which included a long, slow 4/4 time in the opening, a march-like second movement, 3/4 time third movement and, in closing, returning to a 2/4 meter. Some were heard to suggest that Beethoven must have been drunk when he wrote it. Famed composer and contemporary Carl Maria von Weber (1786-1826) reportedly declared Beethoven to be 'ripe for the madhouse.'

Beethoven shared some of the musical traits of the Brazilian jazz composers of the mid-twentieth century: he was an improviser, he struggled to be new—too hard, some critics felt—and he wrote beautiful lyrical melodies of great emotion. As with composers such as Jobim and Gilberto, his music was considered avant-garde, unorthodox and experimental.

Like Villa-Lobos, Beethoven had an intense interest in folk music—having arranged over 150 folktunes for George Thomson of Edinburgh, Scotland. He adapted these simple, but beautiful, tunes in many of his works, such as the Seventh Symphony.

MARCHA POPULAIRE
(Folk March)

Interpreted and arranged by Dave Marshall

Ludwig van Beethoven
(1770 - 1827)

MELODO DE LUA
(Moody Melody)

Dave Marshall

Play the Bossa Nova

Dave Marshall

1. "Cor - co - va - da,"   "Des a - fi - na do,"   I miss those mel -o- dies,———   So -
2. Jazz   and   sam- ba,   Bra- zil - ian   mag -ic,   It's not   a   pass- ing   whim,———   Ri -

phis -ti -ca-ted rhy-thm, Se - duc- tive   rhy-thm, With jaz-zy har - mo- nies. ——————
o   de Ja- neir- o is where I   go,   just to   ease the mood I'm in. ——————

Play, —————————— play, —— the bos- sa   no - va, —————————————— The bos- sa

no - va —————— On   your gui - tar,   Play the bos -sa ho - va.

rit. ——————————————————

Samba de Amor

(Samba of Love)

Dave Marshall

SAMBA SONOLENTO
(Sleepy Samba)

moderate tempo
play slow, dreamy

Dave Marshall

WAKE UP!

SAMBA FELIZ
(Happy Samba)

Dave Marshall

SONHADOR
(Day Dreamer)

Dave Marshall